RUPTURE

RUPTURE

Monique Adelle

CODHILL PRESS

NEW YORK • NEW PALTZ

Dedicated to my beloved children
Elijah, Eliana, and Ezekiel

TABLE OF CONTENTS

I

II

III

Another former slave testified to this practice on his plantation: *"A woman who gives offense in the field, and is large in a family way, is compelled to lie down over a hole made to receive her corpulency, and is flogged with a whip or beat with a paddle, which has holes in it; at every stroke comes a blister."*

- Harriet Tubman: *Slavery, the Civil War, and Civil Rights in the 19th Century*

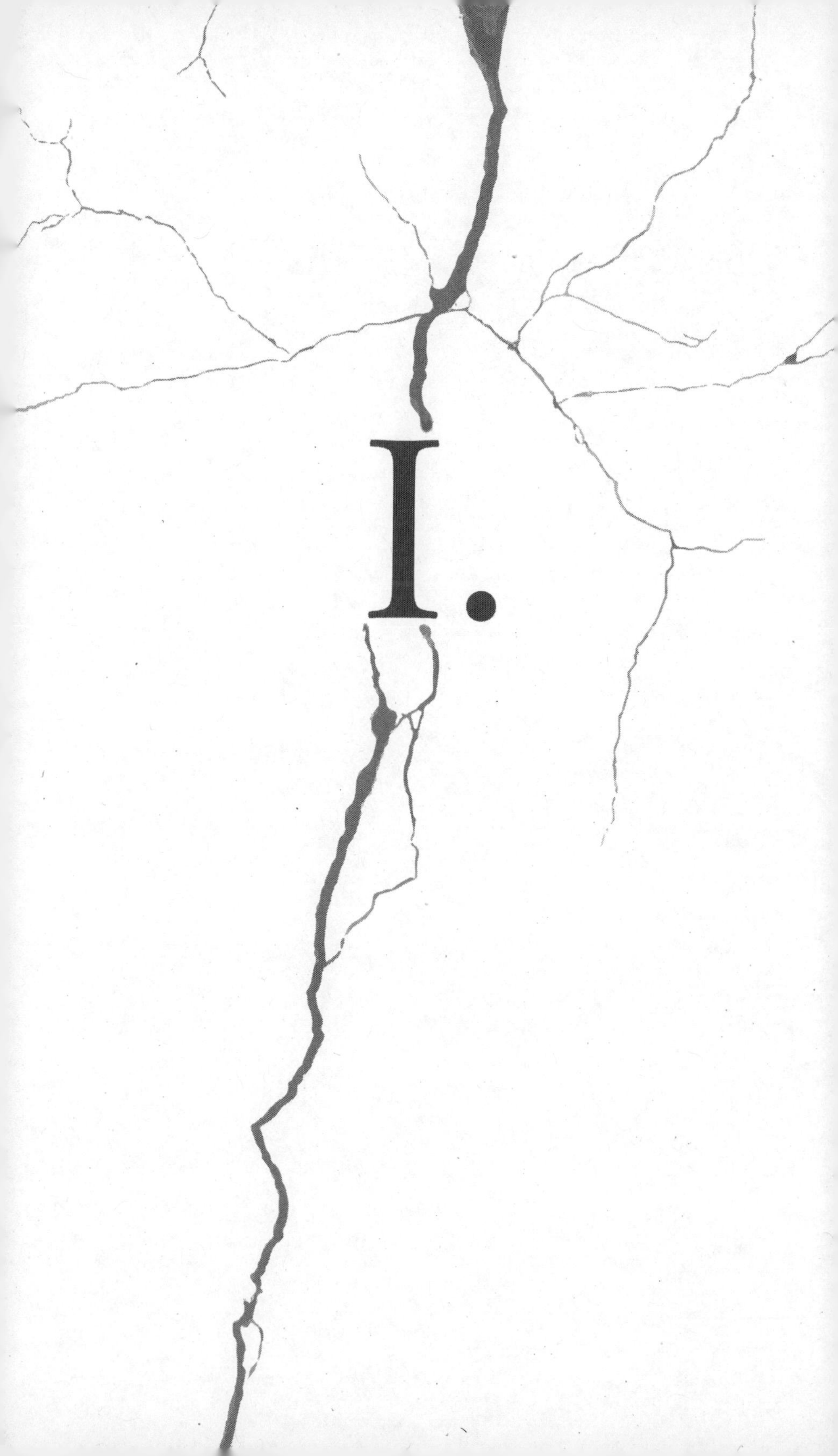

SIRENS

Birds singing clutch branch by claw. Like bow to violin
string, their song bends through trees in a ravenous wood.

The sounds the centuries have made is a music
in the black forest pregnant with birds. These aches,

a heteroglossia. They speak: *Someone
catch the whip tight, beat the trees until they fly.*

NO THING MARKS THE SPOT

where I heave out the afterbirth,
mucilaginous and silent.

The sun is a vulture.
I give it my skin,

a fresh caul of sweat
and stink and love and dirt.

CROWN

a. *To place the crown on the head of she who has been crowned.*
Weighted heft of regalia emblazoned crimson-crested silverings, leaden weight of royalty convalesces at her ankles; her feet permit penitent kisses from broken continents and isles and bent backs like boughs bow, foreheads pressing ripples on the sea's skin.

b. *Crown of a baby's head during labor; to be surrounded by the dilated cervix.*
Mother who has crowned through blood-slick labial folds in thicket like bramble. She who came through great trials receives the crown of the caul cut to let loose her unbreathing child named Hallelujah by this breathless queen who sings and the trees clap their leaves.

c. *To interweave strands in making a crown knot.*
Let the tree hang its weariness over a pocket of sea, branches wrinkled with age yielding to taut line hitch, swinging hovered over anemone and algae. An underworld without time. Kings and queens seated on thrones of coral and skull.

THEY WHOSE TEETH BIT THE COWHIDE

with each strike

their teeth like hungry fingers

of baby boys. Who will cure us

of their speaking

that they may leave us

to our now?

FLAGELLATION OF THE FEMALE
SAMBOE SLAVE

etching by William Blake, 1793

Mark the tree, a mercy in its bent neck, leaves below having
    scurried,
choosing to be fallen. No witness here.

Mark the men. They point in waltz, exhorting those shadowy
    blacks
ordained with sword-like flagellates.

And mark she who hangs, eyes match-struck gaped mouth
in stung whisper.

    Mark the smooth round beginning below her milken
        breasts.

LULA

*Lula Cottonham Walker had to work hard as a slave in
Alabama, according to her later testimony, but the mother of
eight children was never beaten. If the master had a sow that
gave birth to a litter of pigs each year, he would not take a stick
and beat it. It was the same with slaves, she offered by way of
explanation.*

Not sure I could count the ones between the ones I got.

I been blown through the ribcage and teeth. Took like a
    mouth organ an' spat breath
to bulge till full with his or his peak.

I known hungry mouths and razored tongues since I a girl
    plucked canary from my mommas yawn.

Been swollen more times I can count. Some say blessed to
    bargain switch and lash.

Been restless in the way a frayed cloth haunt through a
    howling wind. I been that kine
of not still an' my babies swung-out runts into this life.

By explanation, they keep this mamma's hide clean so the
    only strike be the one struck
clear through my insides, rip me wide, then catch my
    babies in the caul.

HETTY'S TALE

*an enslaved woman in British Jamaica, went into premature
labor after being stripped naked, tied to a tree, and flogged
incessantly by her master with both whip and cowskin. She died
a few days later.*

To own it—
      the cattle prod
        the cow skin,
          her back, neck, calves
            the child in her belly

To own it—
      the fatigue
        of the beating
          she kept on
            taking taking taking

To own it—
      the rage
        the loss
          of the cow the loss
            of the stillborn child

To own it—
      the fear
        of the loss
          of the cow
            of the woman who latched it

so loosely
      it took flight.

BLACK SHEEP

*I consider a woman who brings a child every two years as more
profitable than the best man on the farm…what she produces is
an addition of capital.* –Thomas Jefferson

Every time a Negro baby is born,
Baa, baa, black sheep, have you any wool?
Major Walton gives the mother a calico dress,
Yes sir, yes sir, three bags full. One for my master,
and one bright shiny silver dollar

for the dame. Because Lula Cottonham Walker
gave birth to eight children while enslaved in Alabama—
one for the other man who lives down the lane—
she is never beaten by her master. *Baa, baa, black*

sheep, have you any wool? Yes sir,
Young wenches purchased for breeding shall
do no other work *yes sir,* and prepare for her
a dress, *yes sir,* and she shall wear it.

MARY

Mary Buford did the same work as the men on her Arkansas plantation because, according to her niece, "she wasn't no multiplying woman."

Well, one times one always gonna be one. Yes, my body is

being again a congregation of empty

pews. Prayin' this body stay the *mercy* it be.

ROCK-A-BYE BABY

*Rock-a-bye baby, on the treetop. When the wind blows, the
cradle will rock. When the bough breaks, the cradle will fall...*

See from the treetoptop tree
the wind-blown anemone, see the sea
slap and hiss, take possession
of one more tree in a family of trees,
one more just born into the wet blueblack
winter, one more to sing of, shucked by hands
now blistered with blues now I soothe with sassafrass.

Rock, rock, rock Moses rock, Peter rock, holy sin
passed down pages of passages, tributaries swelling
wet with singsong songs rise to ocean sea billows
roll rock rocking this sweet sweat-earth cradle
til I rise from the mire blowing like last trumps
trumpeting shouts out of Zion.

Down to her knees, down face down, belly down
in the bowl of ground carved to house her swell
while switch swoon against her bare back
and when the bough breaks she bleeds out l
ash by lash by onetwothree   four   five   six seven
eight nine ten eleven tttwwelve
thirrrrr----teeeeen fffffourteeeeen

...and down will come baby, cradle and all.

STORM VIOLENCE

But the wind was hungry
so the earth gave it to eat.

Sky emptied furious palms,
bending the earth to a meek altar.

Where I am, the sky has already spilt
its electric scorch.

Even the earth was hungry
so the winds gave it to eat.

The earth is a body, frenzied boughs
and broken twigs crisscross

this typography; the earth is a body,
wind-torn and giving birth to marigolds.

CASTLE

In a land of bludgeoned castles, my son eats the sand.
An invocation of saltwater summons seaweed

in a waterway. Which of these oceans mothers
those children hurled to a salvation of algae?

A port city's seaways are landlocked
wombs filled to brim with skeletons and glass,

insectivorous city swallowing its citizens
in a litany of anemone. With little fingers

my son builds as I skip rocks over the blue-
green ocean, watching the stones walk on water.

NEW CITY

Ambulatory street hot with citizens
—mouths, eyes, fingertips almost touching.

Bodies swell, hydra limbs like anemone,
a ganglia of statuaries. This city of refuge,

sanctuary for cartographies cut from
parchment, erased of insignia. The ocean is

a synapse. How freely the waterways
dance through the metropolis made

without hands. No nostalgia for land
or its monikers. To summon this city,

to call their names.

HERE BETWEEN

the rough toxins and stinging saliva,
they make cool art with brute apathy

syncopating their fallen music,
a lit match to diaphragm singing.

They become beautiful
body-organs, falling.

A TISKET, A TASKET
Lancaster County, Virginia, 1855

A-tisket A-tasket a brown and yellow basket
Ol' Pharoah Douglass perched Rosetta in his buggy
making haste, for she was, they say, in the full act
and article of parturition; "great with child" was she.

On the way
Rosetta bulged and bit she breached until her body preached.
Eight miles that buggy panted through Virginia woods,
eight miles Rosetta coiled and spat til like a stone

I dropped it I dropped it
her baby boy landed in the cool belly of Ol Pharoah's caravan.
Born alive he wriggled and swooned
slick with caul and vernix glazed. He wailed, Rosetta cried

and Pharoah whipped that aged mule. "Giddeyup old boy,
the going's got to get!" But soon, the cord not yet cut
that tied Rosetta to her son, strangled him good and he died.

A-tisket A-tasket I lost my yellow basket
Rosetta, faint and almost grey around her lips, she moaned
and brayed and pushed the afterbirth; she held the warm blue
body of the boy. Ol' Pharoah pulled his mule to halt.

Rosetta was a hired slave on loan to earn a master's wage,
belonged to Towles and great with child;
he'd sent her off to work that day so not a day to waste.

> *And if the good lord don't return it*
> *Don't know what I'll do.*

RUPTURE

The body is indeed a miracle, its seeds,
its algebraic beauty a perfect capture
of fingers, feet slick with familiar soot.

Her miracle body is indeed a seed, a blossoming
stone-like pit undoing itself of nature
to share its flesh with dirt.

Indeed the miracle is the seed, the body
made beautiful with birth, expectant, a chandelier
brightness in a cloister of fleshy dark.

This body is perfect. This body is petulant, toxic,
prancing proudly towards a life of beautiful dying.

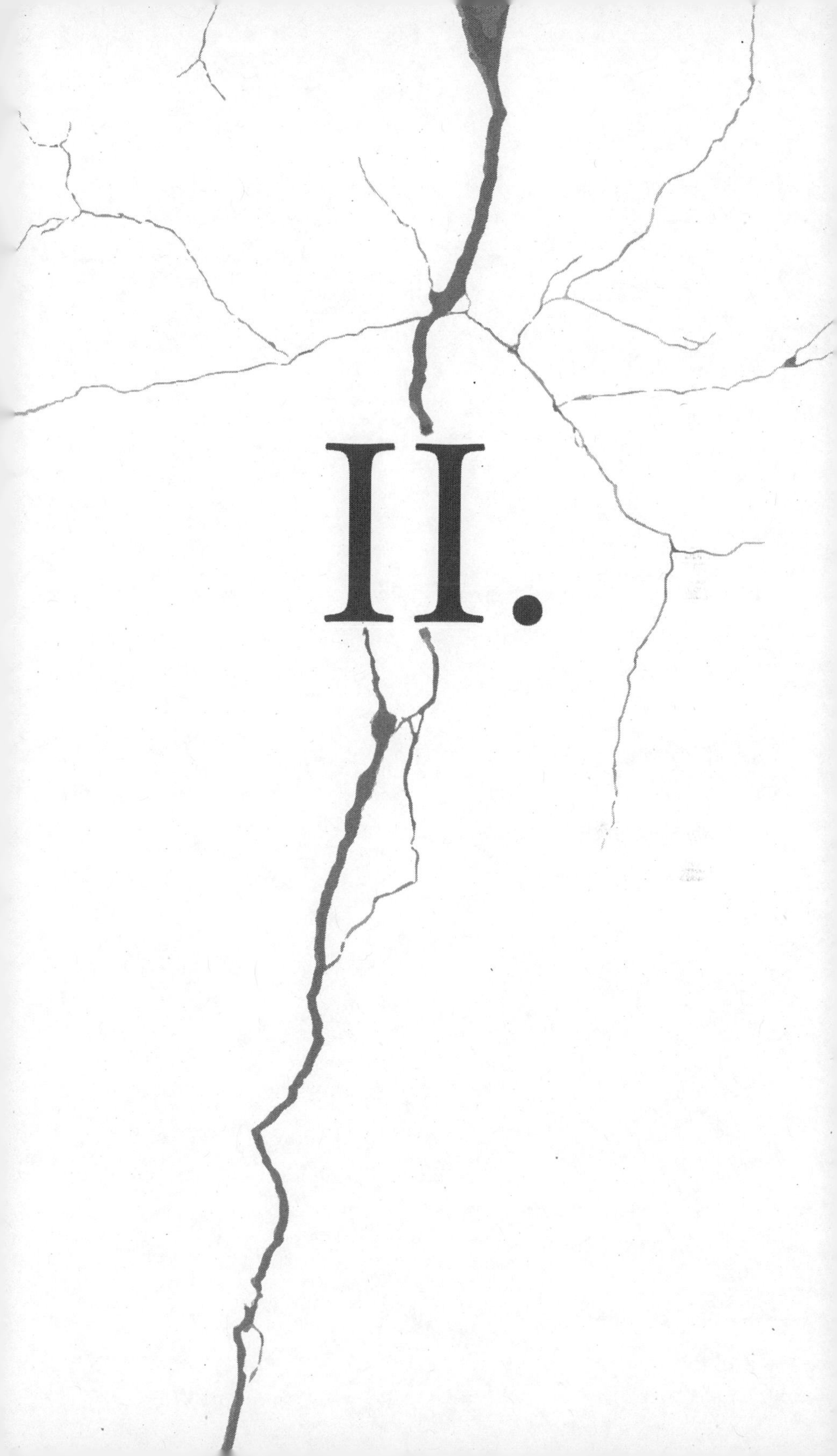

II.

DAUGHTER

Articulate bloom, my Eliana's
        lilac laughter. Clutching

my fingers she buds
        into a fugue of limbs and

wind; she who, after loss
        and extraction, began in me,

now splays her ubiquitous coo—
        damper to the lingering timbre

of grief: a plucked string.

TRACES OF IT

Around our yard until his laughter
    slivers the silent perch

and pinch of winter's chill,
      my husband pulls my son

on a makeshift sled in blinks. A whisper
    of circles etched in

the surface of a deep snow fills in
    with the dust of a

chilled wind's afterbirth. Tracks
    beginning over and

over again, struck by crosses
    of iced flagellum of Pitch Pine.

This coughing of winter's wiles
    holds my husband and my son

in its delight, in its clutch.

THE WHOLE OF MY SON'S BODY

lays on my chest. I lift him
in air feet first, count one two three. We

cross oceans in books from places I've been—
Os cores da Bahia blaze on piano keys. Crisp
hieroglyph of Chinese nursery rhyme.

In the kiddie pool he plants his face open-
mouthed laughing *Eeeeeeeeeeeeeeeeeeeeeeee*
through staggered gulp and cough.

Here, the water cools the wince
of sun's heat pinched between clouds.
Our bodies laugh with touch.

ASK MY FATHER

What is the difference between a pond and a lake?
I ask my father as, on the silent pond, a damselfly
wakes to a wind in the thick necklace of pond-moss.

Rocks and a tangle of birch wood and pine.
Leaves and twigs and other things fallen.
Bristle and patches of grass. The sound of birds

making half-moon dips above the water. We stand
by rocks barricading an end to the pond
and stare out over a green sea, trying to understand

the idea of place, the measurement
of silence between bodies.

JOY
for Elijah

I closed the book! I opened the window!
I let the moment breathe
as loudly as it wanted to. I held it
by the hand, pressed my thumb into its pulse.
I touched my baby on the nose!

I bit, I spit, I swallowed the mangoes
with their juice. I sang, I rang,
I shivered, I quivered.
The whole world opened to a song,
teetering like a bird with wiry feet and wings

that hum through the air to keep it still;
this, the kind of stillness, that moves us.

FIRST SNOW

From inside, I see my husband
and my son making life of blank snow
with twigs in our yard. Soiled
with the cool-hot damp of winter's
afterbirth and the hot funk of sweaty bodies
underneath thick layers of plush,
they coil scarves around their raw necks.

My son is a mouthful of teeth as Daddy
crushes snow into a ball and serves it
like a meal my son eats till his face
is pink laughter. He runs away, I imagine
he will, one day. But, for now,
he runs, just past the window,
through the door, and in to me.

BABY SONG

How this child, jazz of limbs,
can silence to decorum of bones.

How this 3-note blues momma
can make a shuck of her thighs,

lay a song to rest.

NIGHT DANCE

Bathing, she is a slender arc; she is winged;
       we latch—her mouth around my chin;

I feel the spitty scrape of her tooth just below
       my lip. I press my face into hers

She writhes and beats, I break her gently
       against my chest; our choreography

is staccato with speech; her limbs
       splinter the air as if she is flying, no

the water, as if she is drowning. She is naked
       and poised, angled for release

from the snatch, our roiled embrace.

LULLABY AND GOODNIGHT

Lullaby and goodnight, thy mother's delight.
A stillborn to be safe should be delivered
by natural passage. After *bright angels* take flight
the remains will take on the shape of a womb

The womb will contract contract contract
beside my darling until it is again what it was
but not the same. Knowing the body

will continue to elude you
and the next time you think *perhaps*
your body will warm, tender its breasts.
The body will *guard thee at rest* and make

metal of its tongue. And you will say
it is good for this raging body to rest,
to awake without wings *and though shalt*
wake on my breast, knowing the body.

EULOGY

    after At Luca Signorelli's Resurrection of the
Body by Jorie Graham

Not a union of parts but
    an eclipsing of my body
whispering in a silence that is
    prayer. *Is it better, flesh,*

that they should hurry so
    into forever? As long as I am
above water and not
    sea-dreaming green, I may
congregate my fragments
    until they are

speech, a glossolalia of limbs
    singing to a chorus, crest
of an ocean's pitch. I rest
    here; I uncover
the winged specters I want to claim
    as private angels.
I want to believe in the color of

sky. Open and let out
    the air from history's
chamber, dumb with listening
    The earth will be swallowed
if I am silent. In the wreckage
    I find the fragments
of a child—one fibula, one
    fractured tooth, not the stone
        it appears to be.

YOU, CHILD, HAVE COME TO BE

the absence of

shape, a music. Body

shucked of skin.

The losing of

place. An angular listening.

PARTUM

My daughter gurgles and spits
peach-white cereal and watermelon juice.

She laughs her body to pieces.
This may be the last time, they sing

on Communion Sunday, when we break
the bread and drink of the cup.

Just as she is the last.
We pretend we are choosing.

We talk my body—a theatre closing,
a concert ending, the kind of dying that moves

slowly through the body but wakes
suddenly to hush us, like we are children

giggling at the nonsense of dreams.

YOU WERE, ONCE

Like *immaculate* suspends the tongue
inside of its saying, you were, in me.

Like the underwater rainbow bellies
of minnows nipping at my ankle now,

you were conception and yet with teeth
in the throat, a beautiful violence,

a language, even then. As now you *lalala*
your syllables swim delicious in your mouth

like minnows. The pond, too, is agape in wonder
at the sky, the purple evening pregnant with storm.

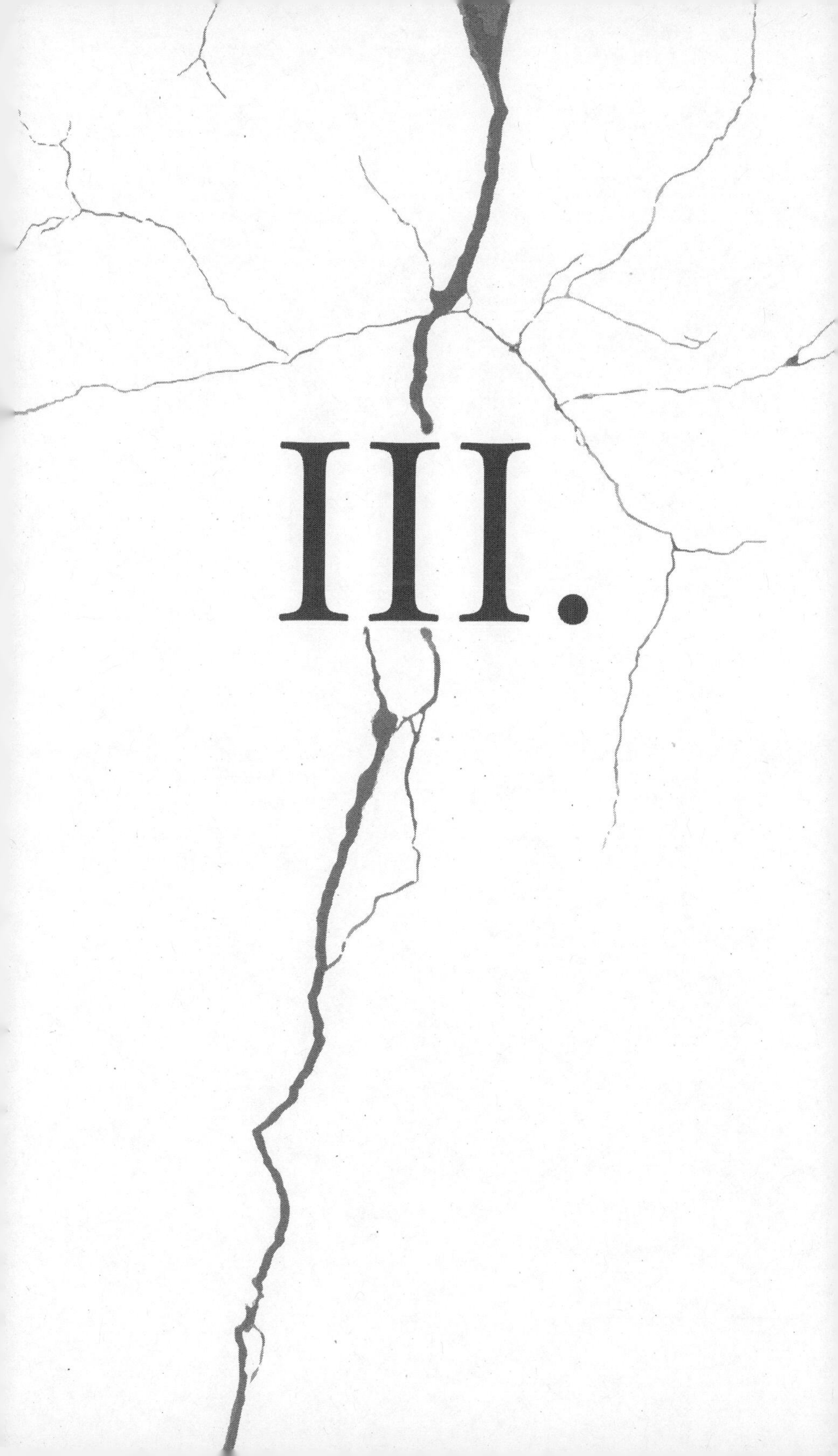
III.

PURGE

a. *To eliminate or expel from the body or an organ.* Throat first then legs coagulated pinprick swelling to a heave-hoe polyphony of muscle chain gang pressing out the body's yolk in a caul. Take this my body. Do it in remembrance of me.

b. *To make pure or clean in spirit, thought, or morals; to free from sin, guilt, error; to make ritually clean.* Wash, scrub to pulp the skin. Make new the roadmap scab smooth it to vellum for this holy writ. Dip one, two, seven times to clean and un-leper the soul of its boils.

c. *To come out of a thing or a place; to go forth.* Marching was plucked from the feet of soldiers and holy shouts, a diction of limbs poised to flee or conquer or been born again, a bright gallop out from tree bellies; birds or bees bedazzle a blank page of sky. Swing low sweet chariot take me and my blue-lipped babies, home.

MAKING VELLUM

*historically the Queen's annual "Gracious Address" from
the throne at the House of Lords was inked on vellum, a
parchment made from the skin of calves.*

Remove the skins.
Soak the skins in water.
Wash. Remove residual flesh
with a fleshing knife.
Wash. Fold the skin.
Pull the hair from the hide.
Soak. Remove the hide.
Pierce it. Use a knife.
Scrape the surface of the hide.
Leave it in the sun for days.
Leave it in the sun for days.
Leave it in the sun for days.
Wipe away debris.
Tighten the cord.
Stretch the hide.
Tighten the cord.
Stretch the hide.
Tighten the cord.
Leave it. Tighten it.
Leave it in the sun for days.
Tighten the cord.
Leave it in the sun for days.
Leave it in the sun for days.
Until dry like dry land.

PASSAGE

Because time is   slow here   and the air
is like gelatinous water.   Sound makes
its mark here and the   staccato you hear
isn't the earth breaking   as much as it is
a woman dancing on water   pulling
                    the sun onto her back.

FOUND POEM: THE AFRICAN DIASPORA

The equatorial region is inhabited by Blacks who are to be
    numbered among the savages and beasts.

Their complexions and hair are burnt; their brains
almost boil from the sun's excessive heat.

They are much given to running away. Dancing and rhythm
are inborn and natural to them.

Their dispositions know no gloom. Their intelligence is dim,
their thoughts not sustained,

their minds inflexible. Opposites such as good faith and
deceit, honesty and treachery, do not coexist

among them. The moral characteristics found in their belief
systems are close to the instincts

found in animals—like braveness in a lion, cunning in a fox.
The blacker they are, the uglier they are, the more

pointed their teeth are, the less use they are and the more it
is to be feared they will harm you.

CUTT

She who is without child,
Carolina planter Joe Fevors Cutt
made like a holy writ, *shall be*

bound to another man.
Starting again from the raw,
my love, I smooth out the scales

of huck-a-berry tree
your back has become.
She who is without child

shall be bound to another
til he presses us out new limbs
to syncopate to cotton-row

rhythm and blues. *She who is*
without child, shall be
bound. To another, your eyes, my

love, silent blooms while Cutt
tries his own hand
at multiplying me.

THE FIRE NEXT TIME

She takes the blackened world's
yesterday between her lips
each word a thrall
in tongue, stammering dance
in fire on ocean, ablaze
with white light grazing on
the seaskin's babbling
with the moon. She speaks
a language of charred limbs,
hung limbs, new and just-born limbs,
now hieroglyphs she makes to alphabet.

FEVER

She writhes, hot, sucks my neck by the collarbone, spits up,
cries, breaks wind, cries, spits up, sucks my neck by the
    collarbone, sucks, sucks.

I hop, shake, bobble up and down and she, a hurled heat on
    my shoulder,
swoons as I bump her bum to the silent music us
is. Her body
slows down to rest, surrendering to a gentle *ssss* sliding flexed
    bottom into the cup of my hand,

head down on my left breast. We sway to what is
no longer her only but I too
have consumed, the beat pulsing in my fingertips
against her back.

I kiss the lobe of her ear
whispering a song
I don't know I know.

I WROTE HER NAME ON A STONE

and threw it into the sea.
    The only way out was up

through the decoupage
    of standstill muck.

In the windstruck trees, a soul,
    in the forest sang

praises, praises, praises,
    joy in this world is

the leaving, leaving, my love, leave.

VISION

A cobra sinks in, teeth to the neck
of a rabbit. Off flits a flock of blackbirds.

A baby slip out into a cotton field,
slick with sludge mudgrass

The royal dead, now wet with heat,
were hanging like fish on the line.

MOTHER

This prayer is in my fingertips, whispering
along the wrinkled path of bones,

crestfallen silk of skin down to where
my fingers touch like an *I love you,*

sweet child, with this my body
breaking. I hold you at the curve

of my neck till your breath sleeps
on my chin; my body keeps on praying

its ache. Every day I am
a violent dance of limbs till dusk

until the body splits to skeleton and skin
and leaves the spirit, alone, free to kneel

at long last before its master.

BLESSED BE SHE WHOSE BODY GAVE

hands, feet, lips that speak
now. They whisper of the slick exit
of the we inside her. It gives way
a surrendered offering for we
who are named. Blessed
be the lamb that was slain
before the foundation of the world.
Blessed be she whose body gave,
blessed be she whose body it gave.

HETTY'S DREAM

In the dream I kill the man,
       snatch the pick ax and swipe.

Dig down deep into skull,
       latch, catch up in netting

of hair and scalp. I spit and beneath me
       a brackish pool forms, warming

cool earth. Someone calls my name
       in the pristine black pitch

of night I swoon like a pelican
       at the noise of a shot.

A minnow falls
       from the thrall of its beak.

MORNING

Contralto hum of a lawnmower's engine
thickening with the sound of scissored

grass, cut off and laying down. A red-breasted
American's libretto wakes bloody summer.

A swarm of gnats in staccato flight,
silent-singing in a blade of light.

THE BIRTH

You survived the calomel and turpentine
I swallowed hoping that you would
find passage to elsewheres.

Because you begin and end with caesura
and hiss slippage into time,
air over tongue, lips open to speech,

a magic, a man in a box with limbs
folded on limbs, like roots winding
around and around in an old pot

a cord connecting body to body
imminent with birth of new
beginning with the sound

of cast iron pot belly boiling full fired up
and blasting the air cool with coughing.

THE WAIT

in this chamber of echoes,
fog-dark swirl of light

on a river, that slices through
orifices of dirt dams, a silk winding

through an opulent earth
seeded with the carcasses of snails.

Here I choose the name
of a child, to be born.

BEATITUDES

Blessed are these the denizens of night songs,
bodies unburdened of skin, silhouettes breathing
imperfect breath in a womb of overturned earth.
We blast through this new aperture, through
a darkroom of human waste. Blessed are we
citizens of this new land of broken staves, wiry gates
released of fleeing notes—a symphony of
rebelious arias coughing through undiscovered streets
while history repeats itself in hungry bellies of men.

AND THE STORY WAS IN THE TREES

The branches are biographers of winter.
Claws clutching ground a tattered aftermath

frenzied with wind; the branches make calculations
of fury, seasonally unbirthing their leaves to the earth.

They lay, motherless, twisted lattices of small deaths
bearing witness. Her mangled back's torn skin—

at every stroke comes a blister—is as the sea's language
of algae swingsinging "she lived, she lived."

To tell this story, the branches must lie, must say
they are waving down ravens or doves, not

summoning the lonely vulture, not
nodding graciously as it feasts.

CHILD

There is a listening she is. A whisper
of Spring's opening bloom, blossom

erecting in a grit-splattered plinth
of snow. She watches the sea—

an aisle of azure. Nagging unborn and blue,
she holds fast her fingers to the dogwood boat,

steadies her body against the ocean's thrust, rises.

REINCARNATION

The itsy bitsy spider climbed up up up
and around and bit the lip of the little one
singing up *up the water spout,*
little sprout, no cooing *ooo* no crying
down came the rain where woozy victims
of heat pluck sweat from wide-eyed bulbs.

Woman with child take to the light weight
of hoeing fences and boiling oils.
Out came the sun dry like a hot wind
wash it out 'til the sun comes to warm
the cool forest leaves covering
these graves. Dig them up again.

ACKNOWLEDGEMENTS

I am deeply grateful for those who helped me work through these poems at various levels: Douglas Kearney for helping me revise this manuscript to its deepest truth, to the writers at Colrain Manuscript Conference where the seeds for the manuscript began to emerge, to my husband Eugene for believing in the value of the work and for making it possible for me to spend time with it.

I acknowledge the editors and publishers in whose journals some of these poems first appeared:

"Flagellation of the Female Samboe Slave," "Lula," "Traces of It," and "Ask My Father" in *Evergreen Review*

"Hetty" and "A Tisket, A Tasket" in *Beloit Poetry Journal*